CONTENTS

World Ecology

www.two-canpublishing.com

Published by Two-Can Publishing,
43-45 Dorset Street, London W1U 7NA

© 2002, 2000 Two-Can Publishing
Series concept and original design © Andrew Haslam

For information on Two-Can books and multimedia,
call (0)20 7224 2440, fax (0)20 7224 7005, or visit our website at
http://www.two-canpublishing.com

Cover design: Picthall & Gunzi Ltd

HB ISBN 1-85434-696-2
PB ISBN 1-84301-093-3

HB   2 3 4 5 6 7 8 9 10 04 03 02
PB 1 2 3 4 5 6 7 8 9 10 04 03 02

COVER
Photographs courtesy of Space Frontiers Ltd (Earth), Telegraph Colour Library; Dominic Zwemmer (rock carvings/ Namibia);
A.C. Twomey (avalanche/ Mount Everest) and Simon Fraser (wild garlic), Science Photo Library.

MOUNTAINS
Author: Catherine Bradley; Consultant: Roger Hammond, Director of Living Earth; Designer: Belinda Webster. Photographic credits:
Bruce Coleman: pp.6–7, 9 (top and bottom), 10 (l), 11 (r), 12 (r), 15 (top), 16, 22, 23, 24; Zefa: p.10 (l); London/ Ian Beames: p.10 (centre); Ardea,
London: pp.12 (bottom l, top r), 17 (bottom l, bottom), 19, 20 (bottom l); Survival Anglia: pp.12 (bottom r), 14, 17 (top); Hutchison Library:
pp.18 (top), 19 (r). Illustrations by Michaela Stewart. Story written by Claire Watts. Edited by Monica Byles.

DESERTS
Author & Designer: Lucy Baker; Consultant: George Hammond, Director of Living Earth. Photographic credits: Biofotos: pp.34 (l), 35,
NHPA: p.34 (r); Ardea: pp.37, 38 (l), 39, 41 (top, bottom), 42–43, 46 (top); Bruce Coleman: pp.38 (r), 40 (bottom); Zefa: pp.40 (top), 47, 48 (bottom);
Planet Earth: p.44; Science Photo Library: p.45; The Hutchison Library: p.46 (top); B&C Alexander: p.48 (top); Impact Photos: p.49, 53 (bottom);
Mark Edwards: pp.50–51; Oxfam: p.52; Picturepoint: p.53 (top). Illustrations by Francis Mosley. Story illustrated by Valerie McBride.

OCEANS
Author & Designer: Lucy Baker; Consultant: Roger Hammond, Director of Living Earth. Photographic credits: Greenpeace: p.62;
Ardea: pp. 63, 65, 70 (top), 72, 74, 75 (bottom), 78, 80–81; Zefa: pp.66–67, 79; Planet Earth: pp.68, 71 (top l, top r, bottom), 73, 75 (top);
Oxford Scientific Films: pp.69 (top, bottom), 70 (bottom); B&C Alexander: p.78. Illustrations by Francis Mosley. Artworking by Claire Legemah.

WOODLANDS
Author: Rosanne Hooper; Consultant: Keith Jones, Environmental Consultant; Editor: Lucy Duke; Designer: Fiona Robson. Photographic credits:
Planet Earth: pp.90–91, 96, 101 (top); Bruce Coleman: pp.92, 95 (top) 98, 99, 101 (bottom), 106–107; Zefa: pp.93 (top, bottom), 94 (top), 97 (r), 100,
102, 105 (l); Frank Lane: pp.94 (bottom), 104; B&C Alexander: p.103 (top); Biofotos: p.103 (bottom); Image Bank: p.105 (r); Still: p.108;
Panos: p.109. Illustrations by Madeleine David. Story illustrations by Ruth Rivers.

Printed in Hong Kong by Wing King Tong

Words marked in **bold** are explained in the glossary.

Mountains

LOOKING AT MOUNTAINS

High above the valleys and plains soar the mighty mountains of the world. Mountains come in many different shapes and sizes. They can be jagged, icy peaks, smoking **volcanoes**, or even green and fertile islands.

A wide and unique variety of animals, plants and people have adapted to life on the steep and rocky slopes. Some insects also live on the mountain pastures. A few, like glacier fleas, can even live in ice and snow.

THE HEART OF THE EARTH

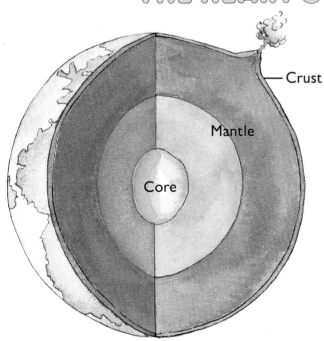

Crust

Mantle

Core

The Earth is like an onion, made up of different layers of rock. The centre, or **core**, of the Earth is likely to be made of nickel and iron. The next layer outwards is the **mantle**, a tightly packed band of rock about 3,000 km thick. We live on the cool, outermost layer, or **crust**. This is up to 50 km thick in most places.

Near the Earth's crust, the rocks of the mantle are hot and molten. This liquid rock is squeezed from every side. Where the crust is weak it spews out the rock or lava, and forms a type of mountain called a volcano.

Very few mountains rise alone from a plain. Usually they form part of a longer chain or range of mountains, such as the Andes, which run the length of the west coast of South America. As the Earth's surface changes, new mountains form slowly, over millions of years, as older ones gradually wear away.

This book looks mainly at the many different forms of life on the mighty mountains of the world.

▼ Mount Everest in the Himalayas is the highest peak on Earth. It is 8,848 m high. The Himalayas are the world's most recently formed mountain range. It is 2,400 km long and 6,000 m high, on average.

MAKING MOUNTAINS

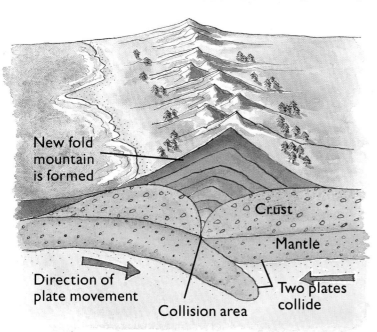

New fold mountain is formed

Crust

Mantle

Direction of plate movement

Collision area

Two plates collide

Large areas of the crust, called **plates**, move slowly around on the Earth's surface. The oceans and continents ride on the plates. Long ago, the plates were joined. Their edges could still fit together like pieces of a puzzle.

Sometimes the plates meet and grind together, causing earthquakes. At their edges the rocks slowly fold upwards to form **fold mountains**, or drift apart to form valleys.

One plate may make the edge of another plate sink, while the rocks at its own edge rise very slowly to make a new range of mountains.

WHERE IN THE WORLD?

Any land over 300 m above the surrounding flat land can be called mountainous. Mountains cover about one-fifth of the Earth's surface. The continents of Australia and Africa have only very few mountains, while Asia has huge areas of mountainous land across its surface.

Vast underwater mountains also form part of the floors of the oceans. Hawaii is the topmost part of an underwater volcano. Measured from the sea floor, it is even higher than Mount Everest at over 9,000 m tall.

Block mountains have broad, flat tops, or **plateaux**. These mountains form when blocks of rock are forced up through cracks, or faults, in the crust by the liquid rock in the mantle. Rift valleys form when rock slides into a crack in the crust.

▼ This map shows the main mountain ranges. The younger ones, the Alps, the Rockies, the Andes and the Himalayas, are fold mountains. The Scottish Highlands, the Atlas and Appalachian Mountains, the Drakensberg, the Urals and the Pyrenees are older and have been worn by the weather for millions of years.

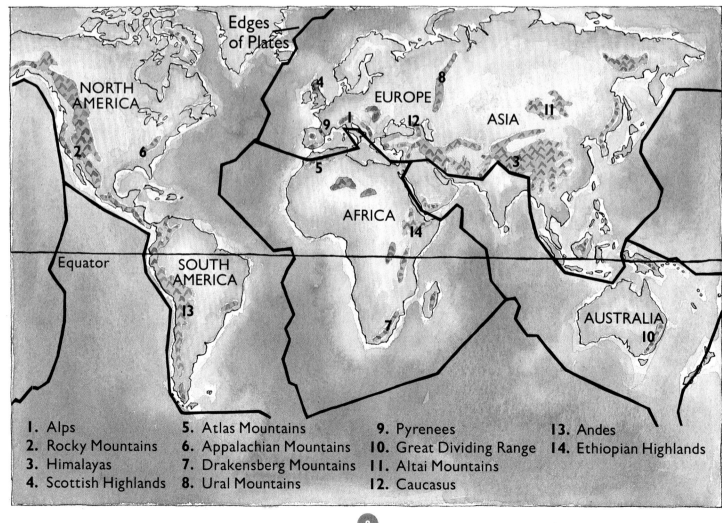

1. Alps
2. Rocky Mountains
3. Himalayas
4. Scottish Highlands
5. Atlas Mountains
6. Appalachian Mountains
7. Drakensberg Mountains
8. Ural Mountains
9. Pyrenees
10. Great Dividing Range
11. Altai Mountains
12. Caucasus
13. Andes
14. Ethiopian Highlands

◀ Mount Augustine is a live volcanic island off the coast of Alaska, USA. In 1986, it erupted and ash and gases spouted from its crater.

▼ Weird limestone mountains stand near the Guilin Li River in China. Limestone is soft and is gradually worn away by the wind, or dissolved by rain. Over the years, these unusual mountains have been slowly ground into strange shapes.

ICE, SNOW AND RAIN

Mountains change all the time. Over the years, heavy rains soften their rocky outlines, and gather to form rivers. These eventually carve deep V-shaped channels or valleys into the side of the mountain.

Ice and snow also change the shape of the mountains. There is less air high up a mountain to trap the warmth of the Sun's rays. It is very cold and many of the world's peaks are covered with a deep blanket of snow and ice throughout the entire year.

RAIN SHADOWS

Rain-filled clouds blow towards the land from the sea. They release their moisture when they reach cold mountain air. The landward side of a mountain receives little rain and is called the **rain shadow**.

▲ Sometimes snow gets too heavy and slips down the mountainside as an **avalanche**.

► Ice may form slow-moving rivers called glaciers. Stones and rocks in the ice **erode,** or wear away, the mountains, leaving U-shaped channels, known as glaciated valleys. The glacier melts as it gets further from the cold peak and into warmer areas. This is the John Hopkins glacier in Alaska, USA.

▼ Heavy rains often loosen the earth on a mountain and lead to a landslide. Strong winds may also blow away rocks and soil and change its shape. Sometimes heavy rocks and earth tumble down a mountainside damaging buildings and injuring people.

TREES AND PLANTS

At high **altitudes**, it becomes harder for mountain plants to survive the cold and lack of water. Completely different plants will grow on a protected sunny slope than on a slope exposed to icy winds.

In the northern hemisphere, both **deciduous** and **coniferous** trees grow on the lower slopes. Further up, the deciduous trees thin out, and the conifers grow more thickly. Beyond, a few conifers struggle to the **treeline**. Above this, conditions are too harsh for trees to grow. The height of the treeline varies with **latitude** and local weather patterns. Mountains away from the **Equator** are colder and have lower treelines.

In tropical areas, dense rainforests grow lower down, while lush 'cloud' forests of mossy **evergreens** grow further up the mountain slopes.

▲ A small Ponderosa pine anchors itself in a boulder on a steep mountainside. The waxy needle-like leaves contain very little water to freeze, and are shaped so that most snow will slide off the branches and not harm the tree.

◀ Cushions of grass, moss and lichen grow on the thin soil and rock of the upper slopes. At ground level they are sheltered from the winds. All plant life stops at the **snowline**.

► In summer, the meadows high up in the European Alps are covered in a rich carpet of flowers. The plants must be sturdy to combat the cold and windy conditions. They are only a few centimetres high and have stems that can bend in the wind. Their roots hold them firmly in place. The petals are brightly coloured to attract the few insects living there.

PLANT PANEL

In the northern hemisphere, deciduous and coniferous trees grow on the lower slopes. Higher up, only coniferous trees survive. Once past the treeline, shrubs, grasses and flowers may grow on the thin mountain soil.

▼ The giant lobelia lives on Mount Kenya. It traps air in its hairs to keep warm. It grows up to 8m tall and has spiky blue flowers.

KEEPING WARM

Mountain animals have long hair with a thick undercoat of fur to keep them warm. They are often larger than relatives in valleys and plains. Some animals, like wild sheep and goats, feed on the top pastures in summer, and move downhill in winter. Smaller animals, like Alpine marmots and the mountain hares of Europe and Asia, feed mainly in the top meadows. Marmots feed all summer, then **hibernate** for eight months of the year and lose as much as one-quarter of their body fat.

Several **predators** stalk the mountains. In the Himalayas, rare snow leopards live near the snowline and prey on grazing animals. In Europe, hunters like wolves and lynxes are occasionally seen.

▲ Mountain goats have hard, sharp hooves which grip the rock like pincers as they move about the slippery top slopes to graze.

ANIMAL FACTS

● Pikas are found on European, Asian and North American mountains. They feed on grasses and other plants. They spend the summer building up stores of food to eat during the winter.

● The snow rabbit and the mountain hare both turn white in the winter so that they are hidden against the snow. This form of protection against predators is called **camouflage**.

▶ The North American cougar lives close to the snowline during the summer. Cougars, like brown bears and lynxes, prey on goats and other grazing animals.

▼ The macaque monkeys in the Shiga Highlands of Japan have learned to keep warm in the local hot springs. They cook their vegetables in the hot water before eating them. Here, one monkey checks fur for ticks and fleas.

FLYING AND HOPPING

Animals living on either side of a mountain range are often quite unrelated. Some birds and insects, however, manage to overcome the altitude and cross the mountains. Birds must have thick feathers and efficient lungs to be able to fly so high. Specially equipped birds include the bar-headed geese, which migrate from Siberia to their distant wintering grounds in India.

The large birds of prey that live close to the mountain peaks include the giant Andean condor, the lammergeier and the golden eagle. There are also smaller birds that remain close to the ground, such as the Alpine chough in Europe and Asia, which feeds on insects, butterflies and mountain plants.

FLYING HIGH

The Apollo butterfly lives on some of the highest mountains of Europe and Asia. It flies only when sunshine warms it. When the Sun goes behind a cloud, it drops to the ground to save energy. The Apollo is now protected by law from keen butterfly collectors in most of its habitats in Europe.

◀ The mountain grasshopper has stiff flaps where its wings used to be. Those insects, like butterflies, that do still fly, stay near the ground so they do not get blown away by the wind. Some insects even survive above the snowline.

▶ In the French Pyrenees a male capercaillie struts about in the snow, searching for a mate. Its call is a series of crackles and pops. The capercaillie mainly feeds on buds, and cones. It is the largest type of grouse.

▲ The lammergeier nests in the peaks. It is a large mountain vulture native to Europe, Asia and Africa, and feeds mostly on dead animals. Most other birds could not survive in the cold.

► The hummingbirds of the high Andes become sluggish when it is cold at night. This is a red-tailed comet hummingbird.

MOUNTAIN DWELLERS

Lowland people are exhausted at high altitudes. There is little oxygen and it is extremely cold. Mountain people have adapted to these harsh conditions. People like the Bhotia in the Himalayas have enlarged hearts and lungs and wide nostrils so that their bodies may take in enough oxygen. They depend on sturdy yaks, members of the cattle family, to provide them with meat, wool, milk, transport, hides, and butter.

In many areas, such as the Rocky Mountains, the European Alps, and Scandinavia, farmers rear dairy cattle and sheep in the mountains. The animals are often kept in barns on the valley floors to shelter from the winter snows, and in the summer are herded to the higher pastures to be fattened on the rich grasses.

▲ An Afghan woman dressed in richly coloured clothing milks her goat in the Hindu Kush.

▶ A lively market takes place in the Sherpa capital of Namche in Nepal. Sherpas farm, raise animals and trade. They often act as guides and porters for mountaineering expeditions.

PEOPLE FACTS

● The Lapps are nomads living in northern Sweden. Some Lapps keep reindeer to provide meat and milk, and skin to make tents and clothes.

●The Andean peoples of South America keep llamas, vicuñas and alpacas. Some mine tin, copper, gold and silver. Others grow barley and potatoes.

MOUNTAIN TREASURES

Valuable resources such as coal, metals like copper, zinc and iron ores, as well as semi-precious and precious minerals, are mined from mountains. The bare rock itself is used by the building industry.

The banks of the Rocky Mountains in Canada are covered with useful softwoods, like aspen, pine and spruce. Hardwoods like teak, ebony, mahogany and rosewood grow on tropical mountains. Ships, furniture and building materials are made from different types of wood.

Mountain rivers are often dammed to feed a reservoir of water. The rushing torrent turns huge turbines which generate enough electricity to power whole cities or even nations, such as mountainous Switzerland.

▼ A dam is built on Columbia River, Canada, to store water for the use of city-dwellers.

▶ A loader piles logs on to the back of a trailer. When trees are felled on mountain slopes, the rain is no longer absorbed by the roots but runs freely, washing soil into the rivers. In the end, the slopes are left bare and eroded. With proper management, wood can be cut from special plantations.

◀ Emeralds are mined in the Andes, in Colombia. The stones are cut and polished to make jewellery.

MOUNTAIN STOREHOUSE

Jewels, such as diamonds, rubies, emeralds, sapphires, quartz, gold and platinum are taken from minerals and rocks found in the mountains.

Granite and marble may be used in building banks, town halls or palaces. Slate is used for making roofing tiles, and limestone is used to make cement.

Copper, zinc and iron are extracted from mountain rocks. They are used in construction and sculpture, and to make jewellery, tools and utensils.

Softwoods are important for use in the construction of buildings, for making paper and as fuel. Hardwoods are used for making long-lasting furniture.

MOUNTAINS IN DANGER

There are many threats to the mountains. Summer visitors can erode paths and crush rare plants. New ski resorts may scar whole mountainsides with cable-cars and ski-lifts.

Everywhere, mountain forests are being damaged. In many industrial nations **acid rain** harms mountain forests. Cars and factories produce chemicals which **pollute** the rain. In Nepal, many trees are felled for fuel. Remaining tree roots cannot absorb enough rainwater, and so the fertile topsoil washes into the rivers, flooding them downstream. The mountain slopes are left bare, stripped down to their barren rock.

Mining can destroy a mountain, leaving only ugly waste. In Western Australia, entire mountains are dug away to remove their iron ore.

▲ In the Black Forest, southern Germany, mountain trees are poisoned by acid rain. The trees lose their leaves, wither and die.

▶ This rubbish was left by climbers on Mount Everest. Much of the rubbish is plastic, which will never break down, but will continue to blow around the mountainside for many years.

EROSION

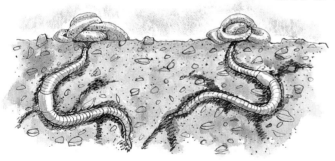

Earthworms help to wear down the mountains. Air and rain travel down the tunnels to break down rocks below. Fragments of rock come to the surface in the wormcasts, and are washed away.

In 1900, forests covered 40 per cent of Ethiopia. Trees were felled, and crops and cattle eroded the bare earth. Today, trees cover only four per cent of mountainous Ethiopia and there are often famines.

SAVE THE MOUNTAINS

In many countries, people have completely changed the nature of their local mountains. In some areas of Greece, for example, the forests have been cut down, and sheep and goats have eaten the remaining vegetation. The mountains are reduced to bare rock as the unprotected soil has been completely eroded by wind and rain.

Some countries have created national parks to protect their mountains. Forests are managed so that when one tree is cut down, another is planted. The habitat of wild animals, plants and birds is protected from damage by people and industry. In this way, mountains can remain areas of great beauty.

All the world's mountains should be protected against long-lasting damage from mining, logging, and the erosion that follows. Mountains play an important role in the Earth's weather patterns and support a unique variety of animals and plants.

▲ The yak, or grunting ox, lives on the slopes of the Himalayas, in Nepal. These animals have long been used by local people for transport and as a supply of meat and milk. Local people must fight to preserve their traditional ways of life in the mountains.

◀ A volcano rises through the pearly dawn mist in East Java, Indonesia. New volcanoes are formed regularly along lines of faults in the Earth's crust, while old volcanoes cool and become extinct.

WHAT CAN YOU DO?

Support ecology campaigns:

● There are many groups which campaign to protect mountains and other endangered areas. Find out about their work in magazines and newspapers, on the radio or on television.

● Tell your friends and relatives about acid rain and mountains in danger.

● Write to the government and ask its ministers to fight to protect mountains and help prevent acid rain.

When you go walking or climbing in the mountains, follow some essential rules:

● Use only the signposted paths.

● Never pick wild flowers.

● Try not to tread on any plants growing on the mountainside.

HOW COYOTE STOLE FIRE

For thousands of years people have told stories about the world around them. Often these stories try to explain something that people do not understand, like how the world began. This story, told by North American Indians, tries to explain how fire was discovered at the top of a volcanic mountain.

Long ago, when the world was young, Coyote passed by the camp where the People lived. The midday sun was shining on the first snow of winter, and all the People were huddled together in their chilly teepees, far too cold to venture out into the world.

"If only we could keep just a little piece of the warm summer sun in our teepees in the winter," said one, wrapping his thick blanket around him more tightly against the draught. He sneezed and looked miserable.

Coyote pitied the People. His own fur grew thick and warm during the winter. Then Coyote had an idea. Perhaps he could help them!

Coyote travelled all the next day to the very top of a nearby mountain. There, in a huddle, sat three fiery creatures, guarding a tiny fire.

As Coyote approached, the three fiery creatures began to sniff the mountain air and look around them suspiciously. They chattered,

"Who's that? Who's trying to steal our fire? Go away!"

When they saw Coyote, the three fiery creatures began to hiss loudly. They stretched out their fiery fingers towards him until he was forced to back off. Then they settled down around the fire again.

But Coyote had not gone very far. He ran off a little way and then crept back and hid behind some bushes to keep watch.

The three fiery creatures spent the whole day guarding the fire but, as night began to fall, two of them disappeared into a nearby cave. A few hours later, the creature left by the fire went to the mouth of the cave and called out to the others.

The second creature soon came out to take his place. Later, the second creature went to the mouth of the cave and called out. This time there was no reply. He called again, but still got no answer. Finally, he went right inside the cave, and the fire was left unguarded for a few minutes before the third creature came out.

Coyote watched all this with interest. In fact, he sat watching the fiery creatures for three whole days and nights. Every day, the fire was guarded all the time, except for a few minutes of the night when all three fiery creatures went inside the cave. This was his one chance.

On the fourth night Coyote was ready. When the second fiery creature went into the cave to wake up the third, he ran towards the fire, picked up a flaming branch in his jaws and dashed off down the steep side of the mountain.

As he ran, he heard the sounds of screaming behind him. The fiery creatures had discovered their loss and were now chasing after him.

Coyote ran and ran, but the fiery creatures were much faster than him. At last, one of them came near enough to grab at Coyote's tail. He snatched at it with his fiery hand and scorched the tip of Coyote's tail white. To this day, all coyotes have a white tip to their tails.

When Coyote felt the fiery fingers on his tail, he tossed the flaming branch high into the air. Squirrel leapt down from a tree, grabbed the branch, and ran off down the mountain with it. The fiery creatures followed.

Still they ran too fast. Squirrel felt their burning breath on her back, singeing her fur. To this day, her tail curls up from the scorching heat.

Squirrel threw the branch to Chipmunk, who ran on down the mountain with the fiery creatures close behind.

It took only a few minutes before the fiery creatures began to gain on Chipmunk. He felt the fiery claw of one of them grab at his back, but wriggled away. And to this day, chipmunks have stripes down their backs from the fiery claw-marks.

Reaching the bottom of the mountain, Chipmunk threw the burning branch to Frog. Poor Frog could not run very fast at all. The fiery beings swept down on him and one of them grabbed him by the tail. But with one enormous leap, Frog jumped out of the creature's hand, leaving his tail behind. To this day, frogs have no tails.

As soon as he had put some distance between himself and the fiery creatures, Frog threw the flaming branch across to Wood, who swallowed it whole.

The fiery creatures did not know what to do. They were desperate and kicked and scratched and bit at Wood, but he refused to give back their fire. They sat near Wood for four whole days before giving up.

But Coyote knew how to get the fire out of Wood. He taught the People how to twist a stick between their hands with the pointed end rubbing a hole in a piece of wood until a spark appeared. Then the People learned to feed the spark with dry grass until they had a flame. The People could now warm themselves and would never need to be cold again.

TRUE OR FALSE?

Which of these facts are true and which ones are false? If you have read this book carefully, you will know the answers.

1. The outer layer of the Earth is called the mantle.

2. The Earth's plates once fitted together like a giant jigsaw puzzle.

3. Mountains cover about half of the Earth's surface.

4. Land on a mountainside facing away from the sea often receives very little rain.

5. Alpine flowers are often dull in colour to attract local insects.

6. Trees can only survive up to the treeline on the slopes of a mountain.

7. Marmots hibernate all year round and lose most of their body weight.

8. The macaque monkeys of Japan have learned how to cook their food in hot water springs.

9. The Lapps of northern Sweden keep yaks to provide transport, food and skins.

10. Emeralds are used to make jewellery because of their rich red colour.

11. The alternative name for the grunting ox is the yak.

ANSWERS: 1. False 2. True 3. False 4. True 5. False 6. True 7. False 8. True 9. False 10. False 11. True

Deserts

LOOKING AT DESERTS

There are places where rain hardly ever falls and few plants can survive, where the sun scorches the earth and strong winds whip sand and dust from the ground. These places are called **deserts**. But not all deserts are areas of shifting sands and intense heat. In fact, rock and gravel cover the greater part of most deserts. Some deserts, such as the Gobi Desert in Asia, are cold for most of the year. Other deserts are blisteringly hot during the day, but temperatures drop dramatically during the night.

A surprising variety of plant and animal life struggles to survive the harsh conditions of the desert and many people call it their home.

▶ Some of the highest sand dunes in the world can be found in the Namib Desert in southern Africa. Sand dunes are not fixed features of the desert. They are mobile mounds of sand which are shaped by the wind.

▼ Death Valley, California, is the hottest, driest area of the United States.

▼ A boulder-strewn part of the Namib Desert shows signs of life after a good year's rainfall.

WHERE IN THE WORLD?

Deserts cover about one-fifth of all the land in the world. There are deserts in parts of Africa, Asia, Australia and North and South America.

Most deserts lie along two imaginary lines north and south of the Equator, called the **Tropic of Cancer** and the **Tropic of Capricorn**. Here, and in other desert regions, dry air currents blow across the land. These dry air currents can blow hot or cold but they rarely carry rain clouds. Consequently the lands they cross are starved of rain and given no protection from the sun.

This map shows the main desert areas of the world. Do you live near desert lands?

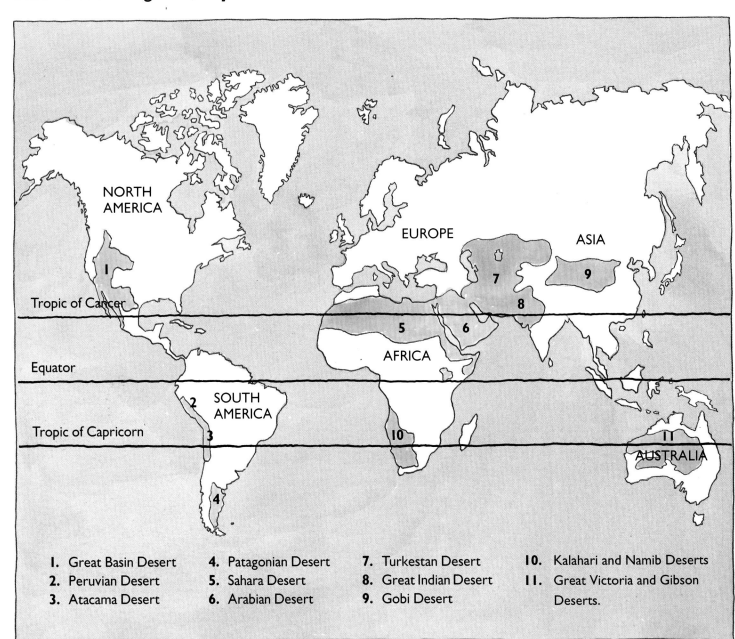

1.	Great Basin Desert	**4.**	Patagonian Desert	**7.**	Turkestan Desert	**10.** Kalahari and Namib Deserts
2.	Peruvian Desert	**5.**	Sahara Desert	**8.**	Great Indian Desert	**11.** Great Victoria and Gibson
3.	Atacama Desert	**6.**	Arabian Desert	**9.**	Gobi Desert	Deserts.

RAIN SHADOWS

Some deserts are called rain shadow deserts. These occur where large mountains block the path of rain-bearing wind. The raised mountain ground pushes the wind upwards and as it rises, it cools. The drop in temperature causes clouds carried by the wind to burst and release their rain. The wind continues over the mountains but by the time it reaches the other side, it carries no rain clouds. This natural process creates some of the world's wettest environments – rainforests – alongside the world's driest.

● The Sahara Desert in northern Africa is the largest desert in the world. It covers an area roughly the size of the United States.

● The Gobi Desert in eastern Asia is situated on high, windy plains. It is the coldest desert in the world.

● Nearly half of Australia is covered by desert.

● The Arabian Desert is the sandiest desert in the world.

● The smallest desert regions of the world are the Peruvian and Atacama Deserts on the western coast of South America.

● Many of the world's deserts are bordered by areas of scant vegetation. These **scrublands** can become true deserts if they lose their native trees and plants.

▲ Ancient rock paintings in African and Asian deserts show giraffes, antelopes and other grazing animals that could not survive in today's desert conditions. This suggests that the lands were once more **fertile**. Evidence of ancient lakes and forests can also be found in the world's deserts.

DESERT PLANTS

It is astonishing that any plants have learned to survive in desert conditions. Most plants rely on regular rainfall, but desert plants may have to go without fresh water for over a year. As well as this, many desert plants have to cope with both hot and cold temperatures as each boiling day turns into another freezing night.

Some desert plants remain hidden in the ground as seeds until rain falls. By waiting until conditions are good, they do not have to cope with the rigours of desert life.

▼ The gigantic welwitschia plant is unique to the Namib Desert. This desert has a rare water source – fogs that drift across it from the coast. The welwitschia's leaves absorb tiny particles of water from the foggy air.

▲ Cacti are the most famous desert plants. They are native to North and South American deserts but they have been introduced to other parts of the world.

Prickly pear cacti were taken to Australia and planted as hedges around homes in the outback. They grew so quickly that large areas were overrun by the spiky plants. Small creatures that eat the prickly pear's soft insides had to be introduced to Australia to help reclaim the land.

▶ Cacti are flowering plants. Some cacti produce flowers every year while others rarely come into blossom. Birds visit cacti to extract sugary nectar from their flowers or search their stems for insects.

The cactus in this picture is a giant saguaro. Saguaro cacti can grow to 15 m (nearly 50 feet) in height and may hold several tonnes of water in their swollen stems. Like other cacti, the saguaro has no leaves. Instead, prickly spines grow around its stem. These spines create a layer of still air around the surface of the plant and so protect it from drying winds.

SURVIVAL TRICKS

Desert plants have special ways of surviving without regular rainfall. Some suck up as much water as they can during occasional rains and then store it in their stems or leaves. Here are some other ways desert plants collect and conserve water.

Some desert trees have long **taproots** which grow deep into the ground to reach underground water sources.

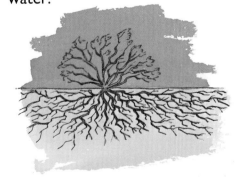

Many plants, like the creosote bush, have a vast network of shallow roots to extract every available drop of moisture from their patch of the desert.

Some desert plants store food and water underground in thickened roots, bulbs or **tubers**. The stems of such plants, exposed to sun and wind, may look dead, but as soon as it rains they spring into life, producing leaves, fruits and flowers.

HIDDEN LIFE

It is difficult to believe that hundreds of different animals live in deserts. Most of the time, these are quiet, still places. This is because many desert creatures move around only at dawn or dusk. At other times of the day, they burrow underground or hide beneath rocks or plants to avoid very hot or cold conditions.

The animals living in the desert rely on plant life and on each other for their survival. Roots, stems, leaves and seeds form the basic diet of many desert creatures and they, in turn, are hunted by other animals. The largest hunters in the desert include wild cats, foxes and wolves.

Some desert creatures get all the water they need from the food they eat. Others have to travel long distances to visit rare water holes.

▲ Scorpions hunt spiders, insects and other small animals on the desert floor. Once they have caught their meal, they use the poisonous stings at the end of their tails to kill their prey. People stung by a scorpion usually suffer a sharp pain, but the most powerful scorpion stings can be deadly.

▼ Some snakes have special ways of moving. The sidewinder throws its head to one side and its body follows in a loop. Snakes can also burrow into the sand to cool down or escape from predators.

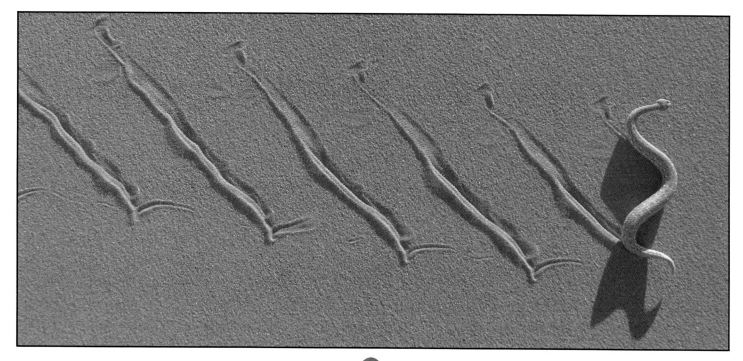

▶ Rabbits, gerbils and many other small mammals live in desert lands. The cottontail rabbit, right, can be found in some American deserts. It has large ears that act as radiators, giving off heat and so helping the rabbit to cool down.

▼ Many lizards live in the world's deserts. Like other reptiles, they have a scaly skin that stops them from drying up in the baking sunshine. Most lizards are insect-eaters. They chase flies or sit patiently waiting for a beetle or a line of ants to pass them by. Lizards have many enemies so they must stay on their guard. The horned lizard, below, has excellent camouflage that makes it hard to find on the desert floor.

CROSSING THE DESERT

The largest desert animals do not remain in one area of the desert. They travel long distances in search of food and water. Small numbers of antelopes, goats and sheep are found in most deserts of the world. A rare horse, called Przewalski's horse, once roamed the cold Gobi Desert but is now thought to be **extinct** in the wild.

The most famous animal to cross the desert is the camel. The camel is sometimes called the ship of the desert because it can travel over vast "seas" of inhospitable rock and sand better than any other animal.

There are two kinds of camels. The dromedary has one hump on its back and a thin coat. It is native to the hot deserts of Arabia and North Africa but it has also been introduced to parts of America and Australia. The Bactrian camel has two humps and a darker, thicker coat than its cousin. It comes from the cooler central Asian deserts.

The camel is well built for desert life. It has bushy eyebrows and two rows of eyelashes to help keep the sand out of its eyes. Its slit nostrils can be closed for the same reason. Its two-toed feet spread out as it walks and stop it sinking into the sand.

The humps on a camel's back do not contain water as was once believed but hold fat reserves that can be broken down into food when the camel is crossing the desert. If a camel is starving, its hump will shrink.

DID YOU KNOW?

● Less than 100 years ago, it was impossible to cross the vast Sahara and Arabian Deserts without the help of a camel. Today cars and trucks are used for many desert journeys and camels are becoming less important to the lives of desert people.

● Thirsty camels can drink up to 140 litres (30 gallons) of water in one sitting and then go for over a week without water.

● The camel is the **domestic** animal of the desert. It is used as transport. It provides meat and milk for food. Its hairy coat is woven into cloth. Even the camel's dry droppings are used as fuel for cooking fires.

WHEN WATER FALLS

Some deserts have regular rainy seasons but others may not see rain for many years. In the desert there are only torrential downpours. Violent desert rainstorms cause flash floods and destruction. Plants are washed away and some animals drown.

Rains bring life as well as death to desert lands. Days after a heavy storm, billions of tiny seeds spring to life on the desert floor. These small flowering plants, called **ephemerals**, have been hiding in the sand since the last rainfall. Millions of insect eggs are also brought to life by the drumming rain, and so an army of flies, bees and wasps appears. These insects feed on the ephemerals and help them to reproduce by spreading pollen from flower to flower.

Eight weeks after the rains, the desert is empty again. The colourful flowers and buzzing insects have gone. But millions and billions of new seeds and eggs now lie hidden in the desert sands. Many of them will be eaten by permanent desert dwellers, but some are bound to survive until the next rains come and the life cycle can be repeated.

▶ Lightning strikes as a storm passes over the Sonoran Desert in North America. A whole year's rainfall can come in one single cloudburst.

▲ Colourful, flowering plants brighten up the sandy Arabian Desert after a recent rainfall.

DID YOU KNOW?

● Sometimes rainstorms fail to wet the desert floor. If it is very hot when a storm occurs, the rain may turn into vapour before it reaches the ground. Over 30 cm (12 inches) of rain may fall during one heavy storm in the desert.

● The Atacama Desert is the driest in the world. Some parts of it experienced a 400-year drought until 1971.

DESERT PEOPLE

The desert is a dangerous place for people unused to its hostile conditions. Even so, a few people call the open desert home.

The **Bushmen** of the Kalahari Desert in southern Africa are **nomads** which means that they travel from place to place. Bushmen survive by hunting wild game and gathering edible plants and insects. Some aboriginals once lived this way in the heart of Australia's desert lands, but most are now settled in government-funded camps.

The world's most barren deserts such as the Sahara, Arabian and Gobi Deserts, do not have enough native plants and animals to support **hunter-gatherers**. Instead, the nomadic people take from the desert what they can, but also kill or trade animals such as goats, sheep, or camels for food.

PEOPLE FACTS

The turban worn by many desert people is not a hat. It is a very long piece of cloth that is wrapped round and round the head. It helps to keep desert sand out of the eyes, nose and mouth.

Bushmen rarely drink. They get most of the water they need from plant roots and desert melons found on or under the desert floor.

People in the cold Gobi Desert live in sturdy, round huts called yurts. These simple homes can withstand winds up to 145 km (90 miles) an hour.

▶ These men belong to a group of people called the Tuareg. The Tuareg were once known as the pirates of the desert. For many years they controlled trade across the Sahara by patrolling the desert on racing camels.

◀ A Bushman of the Kalahari makes a fire by rubbing two sticks together. Bushmen have their own special language that includes clicking sounds. Bushmen live in huts built from local materials. The frame is made of branches and the roof is thatched with long grass.

▼ Many desert nomads live in tents, like the one in this picture. When it is time to move on, the nomads pack up the tent and it is carried by a camel or a donkey.

DESERT OASES

In parts of the desert plants grow in abundance and water is available throughout the year. These places are called oases.

Most oases are fed by underground pools of water that were formed over thousands of years. The water is trapped between layers of rock below the desert floor. Rivers also create oases. The largest oasis in the world lies along the banks of the great River Nile which flows through the Sahara.

Oases are the most densely populated areas of the desert. The regular water supply makes it possible for people to settle permanently and build villages, towns or cities. The land is **irrigated**, and date palms, olives, wheat, millet and other food crops are grown.

▲ If seasonal rains fail, water must be carried to the fields to keep desert crops alive.

▶ Many desert towns are built from materials of the desert itself. Mud is mixed with straw and water to make bricks which are then baked in the sun. This village is the home of the Dogon. Dogon people get their water from nearby mountain pools. The Dogons live in Mali, which is in West Africa.

▼ Oases are like green islands surrounded by a sea of sand and rock. Animals and people alike depend on oases for their drinking water.

Oases do not last for ever. The world's deserts are littered with ghost towns, where the water has run dry or the oasis has been swamped by shifting sand dunes and the people have moved on.

CREEPING DESERTS

The world's deserts are growing. Through a process known as **desertification**, scrub and grasslands become as dry and barren as the deserts they border. At the present rate of desertification, over 200,000 km^2 (77,220 square miles) of new desert land throughout the world are created every year.

Deserts naturally shrink and grow depending on the amount of rain they receive. In recent years, however, widespread **droughts** have caused deserts to grow at an alarming rate.

Scientists believe the droughts are part of a worldwide change in weather patterns caused by pollution in the atmosphere.

Desert nomads speed up the process of desertification by cutting down trees and grazing their animals on threatened grasslands. This leaves the land exposed to sun, wind and occasional violent rains. The delicate **topsoil** dries out, then is blown and washed away.

Intensive farming can also cause desertification. The pressure to grow

more and more food on the same amount of land encourages farmers to overwork the soil, and this can have disastrous consequences. In the 1930s, intensive farming and grazing in America's southern states created a huge area of bare and desert-like land called the Dust Bowl. Droughts had dried up the soil and winds then carried it away. Cities hundreds of miles away were plunged into darkness as huge clouds of dust blew across the sky.

▼ If the ground cover is removed from dry scrublands, the hot sun bakes the earth. Rains run straight off the hard ground and any remaining trees weaken and die.

DID YOU KNOW?

Over 400 million tons of African soil is blown west over the Atlantic Ocean every year. In 1988 hundreds of tiny, pink, Saharan frogs rained down on a British village during a bad storm.

DESERTS TODAY

For centuries, the world's deserts were regarded as terrifying wastelands. They remained the exclusive property of small desert tribes which managed to survive in hostile conditions. Only recently has the arrival of cars, trucks and aeroplanes expanded the possibilities for desert exploration.

Today industries are active in the desert. Mining companies use massive machinery to extract rich mineral reserves such as copper, iron, salt and uranium. Oil is also found in some deserts and has brought great wealth to certain areas. Saudi Arabia has some of the world's largest oil fields.

Elsewhere, modern technology has been used to turn the desert green. By finding new underground water sources or by tapping nearby rivers crops can be grown on desert lands.

Desertification is a problem in many areas of the world, but Africa is the most obvious victim. In some African countries, crops have failed for several years running which has caused widespread **famine**. Many nomads have cast off their ancient way of life as lengthy droughts have left the desert bare.

◀ As rich countries transform their deserts into farmland, poorer African countries try to hold back the creeping edge of the Sahara. This man is building simple rock walls to prevent the seasonal rains from running straight off the hard ground.

DID YOU KNOW?

● Today, **arid** lands produce one-fifth of the world's food supplies. By 2000, one-third of all farmland may be desert if the soil is overworked.

● Satellite pictures can locate hidden water pools under the desert floor. Modern drilling equipment can then reach the water to create new oases.

▲ Oil flares send smoke plumes into the desert air.

▶ Plastic tunnels cover healthy desert crops. The tunnels prevent precious water from **evaporating** into the dry desert air. Continual evaporation may encourage salts to rise to the surface of the desert. These salts kill most plant life and effectively poison the soil.

JEALOUS GOOMBLE-GUBBON

For thousands of years people have told stories about the world around them. Often these stories try to explain something that people do not really understand, such as how the world began, or where light comes from. This tale is told by the aboriginal people of Australia.

Long ago in Australia was the Dream Time when everything was made. The land was made, with mountains, plains and valleys full of all sorts of animals, birds and plants. And the sea was made, full of whales, dolphins and plants, but there were not yet any fish.

All the birds had been given wonderful and extraordinary voices: Crow croaked his rasping caw, Kookaburra laughed her hilarious chuckle and the other birds sang in all their different voices. They sat singing in the trees and bushes all day long, because they were so happy.

When I say they all had wonderful and extraordinary voices, I am forgetting Goomble-Gubbon, the turkey. Goomble-Gubbon could only make a low bubbling noise in his throat, which sounded like this: "goomble gubbon, goomble gubbon". All the other birds thought Goomble-Gubbon's voice was a great joke and they sang even more beautifully when he was around just to tease him.

Of course, they didn't really mean to be cruel. They were all so happy themselves that they did not realise how much they were hurting poor Goomble-Gubbon's feelings. They were very fond of him, in spite of his bad-tempered ways.

Goomble-Gubbon did not find his voice funny. He thought it was terrible and he was very jealous of all the other birds' voices. He tried everything he could to improve his voice, but nothing was any use. "If only the other birds' voices were not so wonderful and extraordinary, my voice would not seem so terrible," he thought.

One day was worse than ever before. The other birds had been laughing at Goomble-Gubbon all morning and he was tired of it. So he went off to visit his friend Lizard. Lizard never laughed at his voice. The two of them sat talking and telling stories until the sun began to set. Just then, Kookaburra flew into the branches of a nearby tree and began to laugh.

Now, Kookaburra could not help laughing. She laughed at everything, even at things that were not at all funny. Goomble-Gubbon should have known this really, but he was fed up with being teased by all the other birds, and so he thought that Kookaburra had flown over and perched on that very branch just to laugh at him.

"What do you think you're laughing at?" he snapped angrily.

Kookaburra looked most surprised and flew off to tell the other birds about Goomble-Gubbon's strange behaviour.

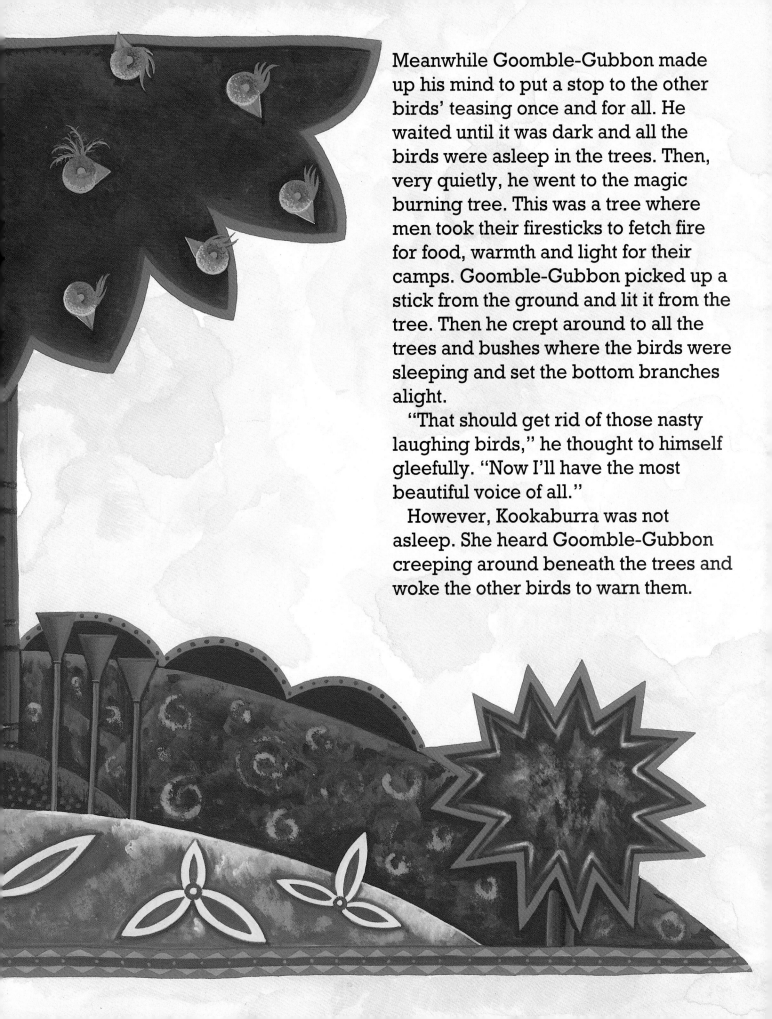

Meanwhile Goomble-Gubbon made up his mind to put a stop to the other birds' teasing once and for all. He waited until it was dark and all the birds were asleep in the trees. Then, very quietly, he went to the magic burning tree. This was a tree where men took their firesticks to fetch fire for food, warmth and light for their camps. Goomble-Gubbon picked up a stick from the ground and lit it from the tree. Then he crept around to all the trees and bushes where the birds were sleeping and set the bottom branches alight.

"That should get rid of those nasty laughing birds," he thought to himself gleefully. "Now I'll have the most beautiful voice of all."

However, Kookaburra was not asleep. She heard Goomble-Gubbon creeping around beneath the trees and woke the other birds to warn them.

A great swarm of birds rose up from the trees, screeching and crying. The birds who could fly fast flew away as quickly as they could to far-off places where there was no fire. Those who could not fly fast enough to get away from the flames flew into the sea to cool off. As they entered the water, their wings turned into fins and their feathers became scales. At last there were fish in the sea!

Goomble-Gubbon was furious that his plan had not worked. He waved the firestick wildly, but only managed to singe his own feathers a nasty smoky colour and burn his head bright red too. He threw the firestick far out into the bush.

The fire in the trees went on burning until the land in the centre of Australia was quite barren and dry. And that is how the desert came to be in the centre of Australia. All because of jealous Goomble-Gubbon.

TRUE OR FALSE?

Which of these facts are true and which ones are false? If you have read this book carefully, you will know the answers.

1. All deserts are very hot.
2. Deserts receive no rain at all during the year.
3. The Gobi Desert is the largest desert in the world.
4. Nights in the desert are extremely cold.

5. Lush rainforests can lie alongside rain shadow deserts.
6. Saguaro cacti can grow up to 15 m (close to 50 feet) high.

7. The ears of the American cottontail rabbit act as radiators.

8. A camel's humps are used to store water.

9. The dromedary has two humps and a thick coat.
10. The Tuareg were once known as the pirates of the desert.
11. Many desert towns are built from mud bricks.
12. In 1988 thousands of large blue fish rained down on a British village during a bad storm.

Answers: 1. False 2. False 3. False 4. True 5. True 6. True 7. True 8. False 9. False 10. True 11. True 12. False.

Oceans

LOOKING AT THE OCEANS

Over two-thirds of the world's surface is covered by vast oceans. The oceans are the oldest and largest living **environments**. Life began here more than 3,500 million years ago. Without the fertile oceans, the Earth would be dry, barren and devoid of life.

Beneath the world's oceans lie rugged mountains, active volcanoes, vast plateaux and almost bottomless **trenches**. The deepest ocean trenches could easily swallow up the tallest mountains on land.

Seen from above, the oceans appear empty and unchanging but beneath the surface hides a unique world where water takes the place of air. A fantastic and rich assortment of plants and animals lives in these waters, from the microscopic **plankton** to the giant blue whale.

DID YOU KNOW?

● Salt is not the only substance found in sea water. There are also tiny traces of gold, silver, uranium and other valuable **minerals**.

● Sound travels through water five times faster than through air. Some sea animals such as dolphins navigate through the oceans by bouncing sounds off their surroundings and listening to their **echoes**.

● Although oceans dominate the world map, we have only just begun to explore their hidden depths. The deepest part of the ocean was first visited in 1960.

▶ There are no boundaries in the ocean. Animals can travel freely through the water. Most sea animals breathe underwater but some, such as dolphins and whales, need to come up for air every few minutes.

◀ In the Tropics the oceans are warm and clear, but around the North and South **Poles** it is very cold; here, parts of the ocean are frozen all year long. Huge chunks of ice, called icebergs, float in these seas.

DIVIDING THE SEAS

In truth there is only one ocean. It stretches from the North Pole to the South Pole and encircles the globe. However, because the **continents** loosely divide the water, four separate oceans are recognised – the Pacific, the Atlantic, the Indian and the Arctic. Within these oceans there are smaller bodies of water called seas, **bays** and **gulfs** that are cut off from the open oceans by land formations.

The Pacific is the largest and deepest of the four great oceans. It covers more of the world's surface than all of the continents put together. The word *pacific* means peaceful but the water can be rough. Waves over 35 m (112 feet) tall have been recorded in the Pacific Ocean.

The Atlantic is the second biggest ocean and the busiest. Boats regularly cross the Atlantic waters carrying cargo between the Americas, Africa and countries in Europe.

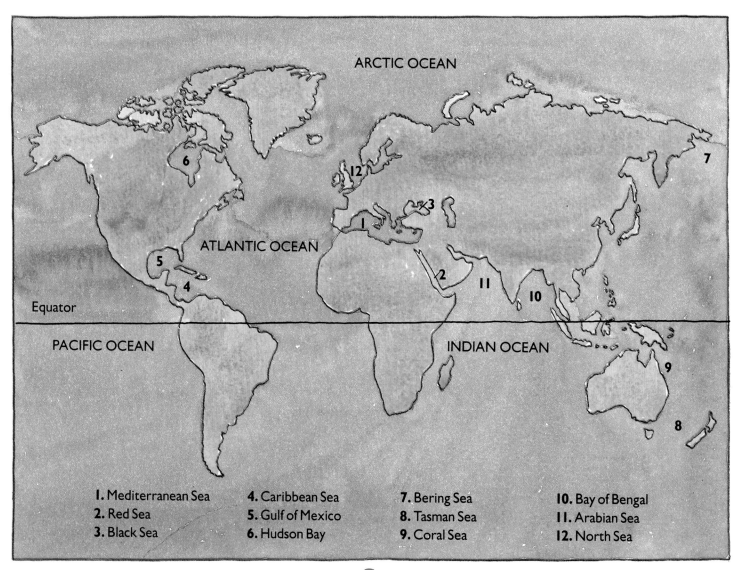

1. Mediterranean Sea	4. Caribbean Sea	7. Bering Sea	10. Bay of Bengal
2. Red Sea	5. Gulf of Mexico	8. Tasman Sea	11. Arabian Sea
3. Black Sea	6. Hudson Bay	9. Coral Sea	12. North Sea

DID YOU KNOW?

● One drop of seawater may travel through all the world's oceans in 5,000 years.

● The Atlantic Ocean is growing and the Pacific Ocean is shrinking. The world's continents move a few centimetres each year. This means that the relative sizes of the oceans are always changing.

● Greek divers are known to have reached depths of 22–30.5 m (75–100 feet) in search of sponges, coral and other treasures. When a diver ran short of breath, he would poke his head into a special weighted diving bell, filled with air from the surface.

● In several countries around the world the legend is told of a lost continent called Atlantis. This land is supposed to have lain in the Atlantic Ocean and was swallowed up by the sea after earthquakes and floods.

▲ In warm, tropical seas where the water is shallow and clear, there are vast, rocky structures known as **coral reefs**. These are formed by small sea animals called polyps. Coral reefs are the **marine** equivalent of the rainforests. They hold a greater variety of life than any other part of the oceans.

MOVING WAVES

The world's oceans are always on the move. They travel in well-defined circular patterns called ocean **currents**. The currents flow like rivers, carrying warm water from the Tropics and cold water from the poles. Where two currents meet, the colder water sinks pushing warmer water up to the surface.

Besides the ocean currents, there is also the regular movement of the **tides**. Twice a day, all around the world, the oceans rise and fall along the coastlines. Scientists do not fully understand how the tides work but they know that they are linked to the pull on the Earth by the Moon and the Sun. The continual movement of the oceans is important to marine life. The tides and currents carry food from one part of the ocean to another. They stir up the water and produce small bubbles of oxygen which the ocean animals need to breathe.

In the northern hemisphere the ocean currents travel in a clockwise direction. In the southern hemisphere they travel anti-clockwise. The wind is the driving force behind the ocean's currents.

OCEAN POWER

Giant whirlpools or maelstroms can occur where two rushing currents are forced through narrow channels. These turbulent waters can wreck small sailing vessels.

Earthquakes and volcanic eruptions under the surface of the ocean can cause huge waves to speed through the water and explode on the shore. These giant waves are often called tidal waves but their proper name is tsunamis.

FOOD FOR LIFE

Plants provide the basic food for life in the ocean, just as they do on land. Plants that grow underwater are called algae and there are two main groups found in the oceans.

The most familiar ocean algae are the seaweeds found around our coastlines. Limpets, periwinkles and other shoreline creatures graze on seaweeds but these are not available to the animals of the open ocean.

The most important marine plants are called phytoplankton. These tiny, floating plants grow wherever sunlight penetrates the water. Huge clouds of phytoplankton drift in the upper layers of the ocean but they are too small to be seen with the naked eye.

Floating alongside and feeding upon the phytoplankton are tiny animals called zooplankton. This rich mix of plant and animal life, called plankton, is the foundation of all marine life.

PLANKTON FACTS

● Sailors crossing the ocean at night often see a soft glow on the water's surface. This is because some plankton produce flashes of blue-green light when they are disturbed.

● The very first lifeforms probably looked similar to today's phytoplankton.

● The largest animal in the world feeds on plankton. A blue whale can weigh over 90 metric tonnes and be over 30.48 m (100 feet) long. It sieves krill, tiny plankton animals, from the ocean waters through a curtain of whalebone inside its mouth.

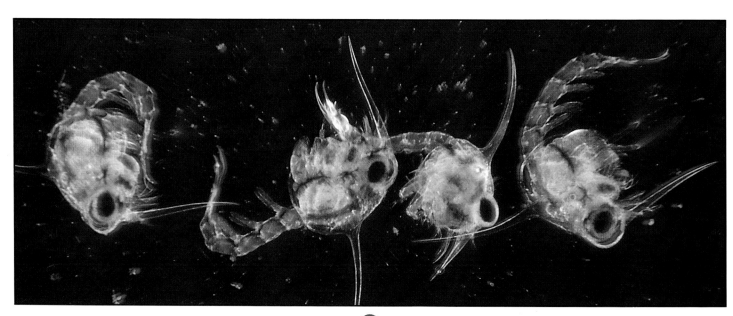

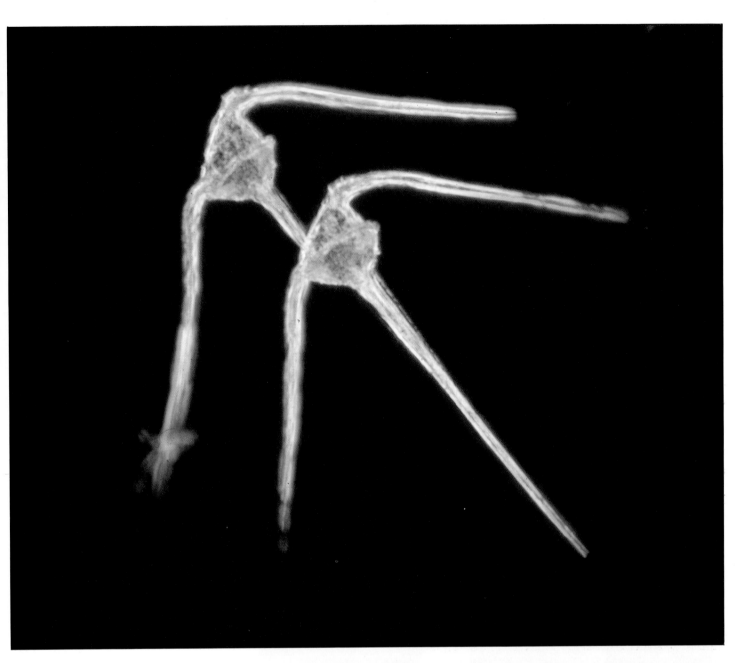

▲ ▶ Many of the tiny floating plants that make up the phytoplankton join together to make chains and bracelets. Others float alone and look like small pill boxes, sea shells, pencils, ice picks or ribbons.

◀ Some members of the zooplankton are simple, single-celled lifeforms but many are the tiny larvae of fish, crabs, starfish and other sea animals.

ALL SHAPES AND SIZES

There is a staggering variety of animals living in the world's oceans. They differ from each other enormously in size, shape and colour. To some extent, the appearance of each marine animal depends on the way it lives and where in the ocean it lives. Sea anemones and sponges, for instance, stay rooted to the ocean floor for their entire lives and look more like plants than animals.

Fishes are the most familiar marine creatures but appearances can be deceptive. Some species, like eels and pipefish, look more like worms or snakes than fish. Others, like the delicate sea horse, seem like a different sort of animal altogether.

▲ Many sea animals are transparent or a silvery-blue colour, but some have bright, bold markings. The most colourful animals live in clear tropical waters. Their striking appearance helps them to establish territory and frighten off would-be attackers.

◀ The octopus is one of many curious sea animals. It has eight arms and a short, rounded body. Many octopuses live on the ocean floor where they hide among rocks and grab passing animals with their long suckered arms. To swim, octopuses squirt water from a special siphon in their bodies.

▲ It is cold, black and very still in the deepest parts of the ocean. Many animals living there have a light on their bodies that they use to attract prey. The deep-sea angler fish, above, is very strange. If the male of the species meets his mate, he attaches himself to her body. After a time, his body breaks down and he becomes no more than a sperm bag used to fertilise the female's eggs.

▲ Sponges encrust rocks, corals and vegetation on the sea floor, from the shallowest coastlines to the deepest trenches. There are over 3,500 marine sponges. Some form fleshy sheets, others upright chimney stacks. Sponges sieve dead and decaying matter from the water around them.

▶ The blue-spotted sting ray is a close relative of the shark. It floats over the surface of the sea bed feeding on slugs, worms and other sea animals.

THE HUNTER AND THE HUNTED

Many marine animals spend their entire lives sifting the water for plankton, but they, in turn, are hunted by other animals. It is estimated that for every ten plankton-feeders at least one hunter lurks nearby.

One of the most notorious marine hunters is the shark. Sharks have a reputation as man-eaters but of the 200 varieties only 25 are dangerous to people. Sharks are perfect killing machines. Their bodies are streamlined for a fast-moving, hunting life and their mouths are lined with razor-sharp teeth.

Not all marine hunters are as fearsome as the sharks. The pretty sea anemone looks harmless but it traps animals in its feathery tentacles and injects poison into its victim's body.

DEFENCE FACTS

Octopuses and cuttlefish squirt ink into the face of their attacker. This gives them time to get away.

Flying fish leap out of the water to escape their enemies.

Many sea animals, like clams and oysters, live in shells. The shells provide a home and act as armour, protecting the animals' soft bodies.

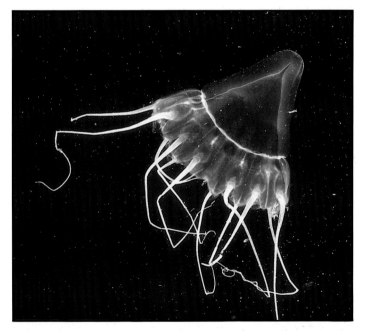

▲ Jellyfish, like sea anemones, catch animals in their trailing tentacles and then poison them. Some of the most powerful poisons in the natural world are produced by jellyfish.

◄ Sharks race through the water, chasing their prey of fish, seals, turtles, small whales, other sharks and even sea birds. Even when they are not chasing their next meal, sharks must keep moving all the time or they begin to sink.

TAKING TO THE WATER

During the long passage of time, a small procession of land animals has turned to the ocean for survival. Reptiles, mammals and even birds have braved the deep, salty waters to take advantage of the rich bounty of sea life.

Whales, seals, turtles and penguins are some of the animals that have left dry land to colonise the oceans. These creatures cannot breathe underwater like true sea animals so they regularly visit the water's surface for air.

Whales are the most successful ocean colonisers. People often mistake them for fish. Whales spend their entire lives in the water but most animals that have taken to the water must come ashore to **reproduce**.

▼ Many birds are called sea birds because they live on coastlines or on remote islands and rely on the oceans for their food. However, one bird in particular has mastered life in the oceans. The penguin spends most of its time swimming in cold waters, chasing fish and other sea animals.

▲ Animals are still turning to the world's oceans. Polar bears are considered to be marine mammals because they spend most of their time on or in the frozen Arctic Ocean hunting seals. They are expert swimmers and their wide, furry paws are webbed to help them move through the water.

▶ Sea reptiles such as turtles are restricted to warm parts of the world's oceans. They leave the water to lay their eggs on sandy beaches.

OCEAN RESOURCES

People cannot live in the world's oceans but they have always harvested the rich waters. As the human population has increased, people have turned to the oceans more and more for food and raw materials. Today over 70 billion kg (70 million tons) of fish are caught each year and one-fifth of the world's oil and gas is mined from the sea bed.

Modern fishing methods are often so intensive that they devastate fish communities and upset the balance of ocean life. Many of yesterday's most fertile seas are no longer able to support large fishing fleets because the fish stocks are so low.

The nets used by many of today's fishermen can also cause problems. They are made of nylon and do not rot underwater. If they are lost overboard, these nets become death traps to seals, dolphins and other marine creatures that cannot detect them.

Fish are not the only animals people take from the ocean. Crabs and lobsters are two of our many seafood products. Sponges are chipped off the ocean floor and end up in bathrooms all over the world. Some seals and whales have been hunted to **extinction** for their meat, fur and oil.

▼ Fishing is big business. Every day thousands of boats drag nets through the oceans to catch fish and other sea animals. This North Sea trawler is small compared to the largest fishing vessels. The world's supertrawlers can be over 90 m (295 feet) long.

OCEAN PRODUCTS

● Fish oils are used to make glue, soap, and margarine.

● A rare gem called a **pearl** is formed inside the shells of certain oysters.

● Big nodules of iron, copper and manganese are lifted from the sea bed using special suction pumps or are raked into nets by dredging machines.

● In dry lands, seawater is sometimes treated to create a fresh water supply.

● Seaweed can be eaten like a vegetable and is also used to help make ice cream, toothpaste, paint, medicine and other everyday products.

MAKING THE SEA SICK

Although we rely on the oceans for food, we treat them like rubbish bins and sewers. Waste is pumped and dumped into the water and man-made **pollutants** such as **pesticides** are washed into the ocean by rivers and streams.

The pollution of the world's oceans is harmful. Many sea animals are injured, strangled or suffocated each year because of floating debris called flotsam. The high level of **toxic** wastes in a few seas is poisoning some animals and driving others away.

Land-locked seas such as the Mediterranean are among the most polluted, but coastal waters everywhere are affected by the waste.

▶ Busy ports can become virtual deserts of the ocean world. The oil, sewage and litter spilled into the water make a harbour unfit for sea life.

▲ Oil spills threaten marine life. This sea bird will probably die unless the oil is cleaned from its feathers.

POLLUTION PROBLEMS

● Sealed barrels of dangerous radioactive and chemical waste have been dumped in some oceans, but no one knows if the containers are safe in the watery conditions.

● In some places around the world the local seafood is unfit to eat.

SAVE THE OCEANS

Countries around the world are beginning to realise the importance of the oceans. International laws have been made to restrict the amount of waste put into the water and some marine mammals are now protected. Countries on the shores of the dirtiest seas have started major clean-up programmes.

There is still a lot to be done. We need to understand patterns of marine life if we are to avoid over-fishing and preserve future fish stocks. In recent years, enormous damage has been caused in some oceans by oil tankers spilling their deadly cargo. Oil blocks out light from the ocean, upsetting plankton production and so affecting all marine life. Through public pressure, oil companies could be persuaded to buy safer boats that would not leak in an accident.

Seemingly harmless activities in the oceans have now been found to have damaging effects on marine life. The electric cables that criss-cross the ocean floor disturb some sea bed creatures and confuse many fish. Sharks bite into the cables, mistaking them for prey. The noise from boats, busy coastal resorts and ocean-based industries frightens away seals, dolphins and other animals from their traditional breeding grounds.

Whales have become a strong international symbol of ocean conservation. These extraordinary creatures have lived in the oceans far longer than people have lived on land. They are giants of the natural world.

Whales have been hunted for their oils and meat for so long that they are now difficult to find.

Most people agree that we must not kill any more whales and laws have been made to protect the largest species. A few countries, however, continue to hunt whales and eat their meat as an expensive delicacy.

DAKUWACA FIGHTS FOR HIS LIFE

For thousands of years people have told stories about the world around them. Often these stories try to explain something that people do not really understand, such as how the world began, or where light comes from. This tale is told by the people of Fiji, who depend on the ocean which surrounds them for food and transport.

Long ago the sharks were the rulers of the islands that make up Fiji in the Pacific Ocean. Each island had its own particular shark who lived beside the reef entrance of the island. These sharks patrolled the waters of their territory, challenging anyone who dared to come near. They allowed friends in but fought with hostile sharks until they paid a tribute.

Dakuwaca thought himself the greatest of all the sharks. He was big and fierce and enjoyed nothing better than a fight with another shark. He had never lost a fight and he was quite sure he never would. He cared nothing for the terrible storms which his fights caused, whipping up the waters so that the islanders were tossed about in their boats. Often island houses were swept away by massive waves from the ocean.

Dakuwaca was patrolling his reef one day when he came across a shark called Masilaca. Masilaca was the mischief maker among the sharks. He did not fight much himself but, with his wily ways, he had caused more fights than most sharks had fought!

"Good day, Dakuwaca," he said. "I suppose you're off for another fight. It's amazing, the way you always beat the other sharks. I wish I were as good a fighter as you."

"No other shark is as good a fighter as I am," said Dakuwaca. "Hardly anyone bothers to challenge me any more. They all know that I am so much stronger than them. In fact it's getting very dull around here."

"Perhaps if you want a really good fight, you should go over to Kandavu Island. I hear there's a creature well worth fighting there, a mighty monster which guards the reef so that it is impossible to go near it. But no one ever goes there because they are much too afraid of the creature," said Masilaca, with a sly glint in his eye. "Of course, I'm not suggesting that you're frightened, you're much too brave and strong. And I'm sure none of the other sharks think that you're afraid either."

Dakuwaca thrashed his tail through the water. Of course he wasn't afraid, what a suggestion! But if the other sharks thought he was afraid, he had better do something at once. Almost before Masilaca had finished speaking, Dakuwaca set off towards Kandavu, determined to challenge the fearsome monster.

As Dakuwaca approached Kandavu, he heard a deep, powerful voice calling from the shore. Dakuwaca had never heard anything like it before, and he found himself trembling a little.

"How foolish," he told himself. "Nothing on the shore can harm me." And he swam on.

"Stop!" commanded the voice. "I am Tui Vesi, the guardian of Kandavu. How dare you approach my precious island so boldly."

Dakuwaca was rather frightened, but determined not to show it.

"And I am Dakuwaca, the greatest of all sharks. Come out and fight to defend your island."

"I am a land guardian and so cannot come into the water to fight you," said Tui Vesi. "I shall send one of my servants to fight you instead. But be warned! It is a great and terrible monster, and it would be much better if you left now."

"No one is braver or stronger than I," said Dakuwaca. "I am not afraid of anything. I will fight your servant."

He swam around the mouth of the reef, watching and waiting for his opponent. His body was strong and quick and his teeth were sharp.

Suddenly a giant arm appeared from the reef and grabbed him. A giant octopus! This wasn't what Dakuwaca was expecting at all! He thrashed and twisted to rid himself of the arm. His sharp teeth were quite useless because he could not bend his body to bite at the arm. The arm loosened as he twisted and, for a moment, Dakuwaca thought he was free. But no, two more arms whipped round, so that he could no longer move at all. And the arms began to squeeze, tighter and tighter until Dakuwaca could bear it no longer.

"Have mercy!" he gasped. "Forgive my terrible presumption, Tui Vesi."

The arms of the octopus loosened slightly, and Tui Vesi's mighty voice boomed out into the waters once more.

"I will release you, Dakuwaca, providing that you promise to guard the people of my island from sharks which might attack them when they go out in their canoes."

"Yes, yes! Of course I will," Dakuwaca agreed.

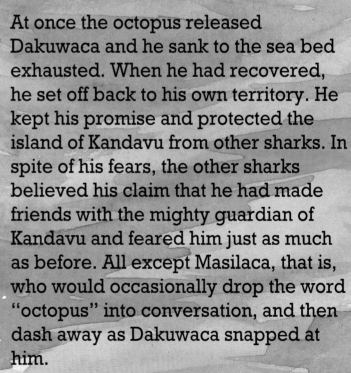

At once the octopus released Dakuwaca and he sank to the sea bed exhausted. When he had recovered, he set off back to his own territory. He kept his promise and protected the island of Kandavu from other sharks. In spite of his fears, the other sharks believed his claim that he had made friends with the mighty guardian of Kandavu and feared him just as much as before. All except Masilaca, that is, who would occasionally drop the word "octopus" into conversation, and then dash away as Dakuwaca snapped at him.

And that is why, while other fishermen of the Fiji islands fear for their lives because of the sharks, the men of Kandavu ride happily in their canoes.

TRUE OR FALSE?

Which of these facts are true and which ones are false? If you have read this book carefully, you will know the answers.

1. Almost one-third of the world's surface is covered by oceans.

2. Dolphins and whales can stay underwater for several hours.

3. Sound travels through water five times faster than through air.

4. The world's four oceans are the Pacific, the Atlantic, the Mediterranean and the Aegean.

5. It takes 5,000 years for one drop of seawater to travel through all the world's oceans.

6. Tsunamis are caused by underwater volcanic eruptions and earthquakes.

7. Plankton is a rich mixture made up of debris from seaweed.

8. Blue whales are the largest animals in the world.

9. Octopuses have 12 arms and feed mainly on seals.

10. Sharks must keep moving all the time or they will sink.

11. Fish travel in schools until they have learnt how to protect themselves.

12. The paws of a polar bear are webbed.

13. Seaweed is used to help make ice cream.

Woodlands

LOOKING AT WOODLANDS

Woodlands are rich in animal and plant life. Trees especially keep the forest alive by providing food and sheltered **habitats** for wildlife.

There are many kinds of woodland which are usually named after the type of trees that grow there. **Deciduous** forests have broadleaved trees such as oak, maple and beech. They lose their leaves in winter and change colour with the seasons.

Coniferous forests are **evergreen**, with trees such as pines and firs. They have needle-shaped leaves which stay on the branches all year round. **Mixed woodlands** contain both coniferous and deciduous trees.

Temperate **rainforests** are warm and damp, but less so than tropical rainforests. They are very rich in unusual **species**, including the giant redwood trees of North America.

A TREE'S LIFE STORY

We can tell the age of a tree by the number of growth rings it has. Most trees grow a new layer of wood each year. Each layer makes another ring which we can see when a tree trunk is cut through. Some ancient bristlecone pines in North America have nearly 5,000. The rings record hot, cold and wet weather, pollution and disease. Scientists can use them to learn about the climate and conditions in ancient times.

WHERE IN THE WORLD?

Since most land is in the northern half of the world, this is where woods and forests are mainly found. They lie between the cold Arctic and the hot, humid tropics. A band of coniferous forests runs across the north from Alaska to Siberia. Deciduous forests grow throughout North America, Europe and Asia. Mixed woodlands grow in some of these areas, too. There are pockets of temperate rainforest in America, China, Japan and New Zealand, while tropical rainforests grow near the Equator.

▶ In deciduous forests, the leaves on the trees lose their green colour, dry out and fall in autumn.

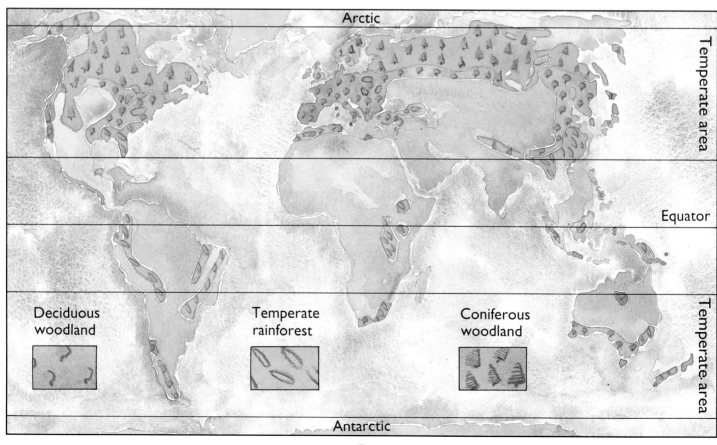

Arctic

Temperate area

Equator

Deciduous woodland

Temperate rainforest

Coniferous woodland

Temperate area

Antarctic

▲ The mountains in the North American state of Colorado have mixed woodland. Deciduous trees show their bright autumn colours while snow covers the conifers.

◀ Temperate rainforests have some of the world's tallest trees. Black bears, black-tailed deer and the tiniest moles also live there.

Until a few hundred years ago, most of Europe and North America was covered with forest. People said that a squirrel could cross a whole **continent** without touching the ground. Today, only a fraction of that woodland is left. Much disappeared to make way for farming and building. The original **wildwoods** are now rare, although areas do still exist, for example in Poland, France, Britain and North America.

SEASONAL CYCLES

Life in a wood is always changing. In early spring, the days grow longer and warmer. **Migrating** birds arrive and build their nests. Flowers appear on the woodland floor. The first of the baby animals are born and feed on the new green leaves so that they can grow strong before the cold weather comes. Sometimes animals have a second family to make sure that some survive. When the summer comes, the forest buzzes with activity. Insects hatch out and woodland creatures feast on the nuts and fruits growing around them.

▲ The forest floor sometimes looks bare because leaves and branches block out the light. Few plants can survive in the dark, shady area below.

◀ Most woodland flowers, such as these bluebells and red campions, bloom in late spring and early summer. They have to make the most of the sunlight to help them grow before the leaves on the trees open out fully and cast a shadow over them. The range of species of flowers growing in an area of woodland can tell us about its age. Older woods often have a much wider variety than young ones and there are some species that can only be found in ancient woodlands.

Woodland creatures such as hedgehogs, dormice and woodchucks hibernate through the winter. They curl up into a tight ball and stay fast asleep. Their bodies cool down to save energy. Squirrels, bears and badgers doze during the cold months, waking and moving around from time to time. Squirrels nibble nuts they stored in the autumn.

▼ The coats of some deer species change colour with the seasons to help them stay hidden from **predators** when the landscape around them changes. Stoats also change, from brown coats in the summer to white 'ermine' coats in the winter.

Gradually the days grow shorter and colder and trees prepare for the winter, changing colour then shedding their leaves. Animals grow thick coats and gather food to last until spring. Some animals **hibernate** to escape the cold. Many species of birds migrate to warmer lands. Snow covers young plants like a blanket to protect them from the harmful frost. In the spring, the cycle begins again.

LEAF LIFE

Trees are a source of life for all the plants and animals in a wood. They are **ecosystems** in themselves. The oak tree alone offers food and shelter to over 300 species of insects. Most woodland trees grow from nuts dispersed by animals or, like other woodland plants, from seeds carried by the wind. This is why woodland flowers like forget-me-nots are so small and hidden. They do not need to attract insects or birds to help them reproduce.

▶ American leaf-cutting ants take pieces from leaves into their nests. They use the leaves to fertilize the tiny fungus on which they feed.

LIFE IN A LOG

Nothing is wasted in a wood. A fallen log lying on the forest floor gives food to other living things and is soon humming with new life. First the slugs and woodlice arrive. They are eaten by centipedes and spiders. A year or so later fungi, mosses and flowers coat the bark. Beetles chew into the wood and reptiles such as lizards, salamanders and snakes lie in wait for them. By the following year, hundreds of insects are busy laying eggs and storing food. Birds come to feed on them. Finally, the insects help the log to crumble and it becomes part of the soil and helps new trees and other plants to grow.

Each species of tree grows best in a particular kind of soil and climate. Ancient oaks are at home in western Europe, as are beeches. These also grow in North America, along with giant redwoods and maples. In Russia and Canada, pines, larches and other conifers make up the biggest forests in the world. Massive kauri trees are native to New Zealand, where Maori people used to make war canoes from them.

▲ The needles on a pine tree help it during the winter. When the ground is frozen, no water gets to the trunk through the roots. Instead, the needles have a coating of wax to keep water inside them from escaping. The shape of the needles makes it difficult for snow to settle on the branches. Their dark colour also helps to absorb extra warmth from the sun.

▲ Many forest trees produce fruits and berries. These make a good meal for insects and birds such as the cedar waxwings of North America. People also eat some woodland fruits and can make use of every part of a tree, even the bark. Oak bark is sometimes used as a medicine for sore throats and nosebleeds, while witch hazel can soothe cuts and bruises.

FO REST BIRDS

Each woodland bird has its favourite niche or place in the forest. Eagles and hawks keep a lookout high in the branches. Owls and nuthatches peer out of old tree holes and capercaillie rummage about on the forest floor. In spring, the forest hums with birdsong from dawn to dusk. This is how birds claim their **territory** and attract a mate. Some give their mate a special **courtship display**. Waxwings give each other 'presents', while male scarlet tanagers have bright, eyecatching red feathers.

Adult birds are always busy. They need to feed their chicks every few hours. Some have adapted specially to forest foods. Crossbills hook pine nuts out of cones with their unusual crossed-over beaks. Nutcrackers wedge nuts in crevices and drill out the kernel. They store nuts for the winter but sometimes forget where they left them. Woodpeckers eat ants in summer and pine cones in winter. Nuthatches can stand upside down on tree trunks to catch insects. Sapsuckers trap insects in tree sap.

WINTER HOLIDAYS

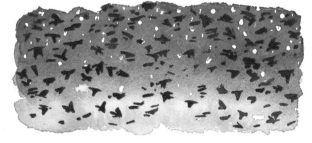

Some birds migrate to escape the cold winter. Warblers steer by the stars to find their way, while thrushes follow the sun. Young cuckoos fly all the way to Africa without their parents. They all fly back again the following spring to build their nests.

◀ Woodpeckers use their beaks like high-speed drills to make holes in trees for nesting or hunting for food. They have very long, sticky tongues which they keep curled up inside their heads. When they have made a hole in the bark or wood of a tree, they use their tongues to reach right inside and pick up insects.

▼ Tawny owls feed on mice and voles which they catch from the forest floor and surrounding countryside. But they are under threat because their woodland habitat has been destroyed in many places, forcing them to hunt in towns and near busy roads.

FOREST VEGETARIANS

Trees provide a larder for thousands of forest creatures. Insect **larvae** burrow into wood. Caterpillars chew leaf edges. Plant bugs suck tree sap. Deer, moose, rabbits and hares munch new green shoots. In winter they switch to nuts, berries and bark, along with squirrels and wild boar. Worms and mites working away deep in the forest floor transform the dead leaves which fall in the autumn into new soil for the following spring.

▶ Beavers are expert engineers. They cut down whole trees with their sharp teeth to build dams and lodges, where they live. These have an underwater entrance to stop predators from getting in. Each part of the dam and lodge is built to make sure there will be no flooding.

FIGHTING FACTS

● Male deer fight 'duels' in the breeding season. They use their antlers as weapons. The strongest one wins a whole herd of female deer to mate with.

● When in danger, a squirrel can stay quite still for half an hour. It warns its family by thumping its feet and slapping its tail on the ground. If it is in a tree when an enemy is near, it drops down to a safe lower branch.

▶ Moose feed on leaves, tree shoots, twigs and grasses. They have very soft, pliable lips and long muzzles which they use to pick delicately at juicy leaves from high branches. They often bend young trees by pushing against the trunks as they reach up for the tender leaves growing at the top. They also eat plants from the bottom of forest lakes and prefer to live in swampy woodland areas.

▼ Chipmunks belong to the same family as squirrels. They burrow underground and build their nests in tunnels. Here they store food such as seeds and nuts to last through their winter hibernation.

Many plant-eating woodland insects are very secretive to avoid predators. The female sawfly hides her eggs in pine needles. She slices the needles open with special 'saws' on her legs and lays her eggs inside. Weevils roll leaves up into a special tube for their eggs. Other insects disguise themselves to look like buds, bird droppings, twigs or dead leaves to fool their enemies.

FOREST HUNTERS

Big forest **carnivores** are becoming rare. There are more of them in the coniferous forests of the north because they are further from the people who affect their woodland environment. Bears and wolves have suffered badly from the loss of large areas of forest which have been cleared to make room for new buildings or farmland.

Lynx and wild cats sit high in the trees ready to pounce on small **rodents**. Wolves hunt together in packs for caribou, moose and deer. They waste nothing and may bury leftovers for another day.

▼ Like badgers, wolves and bats, foxes usually wait until dark to venture out of their dens to hunt. When cubs are a few weeks old, their mother takes them out for hunting lessons.

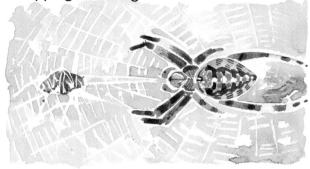

▲ Northern European forest dwellers such as the Lapp or Saami people herd reindeer as part of their traditional way of life. But now some of the forests where they spend the winter are threatened by logging companies.

◀ Bears love to eat fish and wait in streams for salmon to leap out of the water. They also climb trees to raid insect nests searching for honey.

There were once many groups of **nomadic** forest people, such as **native** North American Indians who hunted moose, deer and beaver. A few still live as their ancestors did but many were driven out by European settlers. The forests where they used to live are now being destroyed by developers who plan to exploit their **resources**.

WOODLAND RESOURCES

We all depend on the forest. In the north of the world, we use wood to make our lives comfortable. Many things that we use every day, from tables and chairs to pianos and guitars, begin life as a tree. We turn wood into paper, then into books, newspapers and even babies' nappies. Some of us use as many as 100 sheets of paper each in a day. In the south of the world, wood is essential to survive. Half of all the trees cut down are used for fuel.

All sorts of fruits, nuts, seeds and spices come from the world's forests. Chestnuts and hazelnuts grow in deciduous woods. Apple, apricot, peach and plum trees are traditional woodland species. Today, they are cultivated and the fruits are sold fresh or dry. The sap from maple trees makes maple syrup and juniper berries are used in gin.

However, we take very little food from the forest compared to the quantity of wood we use.

▼ This Gambian woman carries home a supply of wood which she will burn for warmth, cooking food and heating water.

CORK FACTS

Cork comes from the bark of the cork oak tree. It is only stripped off once every 10 years to allow the tree to grow a new layer. When the bark is dry it is processed to make floor tiles and corks for bottles.

▲ The simple pine tree brings us pine nuts, paper, glue and perfumes. In Greece, 'retsina' wine is also made from the resin.

As well as being an important resource for people, woodlands house millions of unique plants and animals. They also hold the soil in place so it does not wash away. They provide moisture for rain and they help to keep our climate steady.

▲ Paper comes from coniferous trees like spruce, pine and larch. Millions are cut down every year. The wood is chopped up, pulped, mixed with water and spread out into sheets to dry. These are used to make newspaper, books, packaging and many other paper products.

SHRINKING WOODS

It is not just tropical rainforests which are disappearing today. Ancient woodlands are going too. In Canada, two thirds of the forest have already vanished. In North America, only one tree in every 20 is spared.

Half of Britain's wildwoods have disappeared in the last century. Beavers, bears and lynx went with them. In Scandinavia, many of the

newly planted forests contain only one tree species.

Trees are cut down to make way for homes, farming and industry. Some are destroyed by forest fires, others by storms. 'Acid rain' caused by factory fumes kills trees and pollutes the soil, rivers and lakes. Germany's white fir trees have been damaged in this way. Hunting, too, endangers animals. For example, there are very few bison now left living wild in the world.

The results are serious. Rare plants and animals are losing their habitat. Soil is **eroding**, climate patterns are changing and droughts and floods are increasing as the world gradually heats up. We need to act now. Our future depends on it.

DID YOU KNOW...?

● When logging companies cut down trees in North America, a quarter of them are unused and are left on the ground to rot.

● Since 1950, over half the world's trees have disappeared and many species are now under threat.

● We are losing 68 species of wildlife every day. By the year 2000, one in every six will have gone. Not since the time of the dinosaurs have so many unique species disappeared every day.

SAVE OUR WOODS

All over the world, people are working to protect woodlands and their wildlife. Environmental groups are campaigning to save endangered species. The sable used to be killed for its hair which was used to make paintbrushes but it has now been saved from **extinction**. National Parks in many places allow animals to live and breed in peace. People are not allowed to hunt or light fires in these areas.

But we need to take more care. In Sweden and Finland, more trees are planted than cut down. But only one or two species are planted, so wildlife is suffering because it needs a variety of trees to make up its true habitat. If we doubled the amount of paper we recycle, we could halve the number of trees we cut down and help to preserve the rich, ancient forests that remain. Governments need to take urgent action to reduce pollution from factories and farms and prevent further **deforestation** and loss of species. They could also encourage **conservation**.

▲ Some Hindus in parts of India hold special ceremonies when they offer gifts to trees to show their respect for nature and living things.

◀ Tree planting schemes are now being set up in every country. These children in Sri Lanka are taking seedlings to a tree nursery to plant.

The Chipko Movement was started by a group of Indian women who saved their forest from loggers by hugging the trees. When the axemen came, the women surrounded the trunks and refused to move. They explained how the trees prevent the soil from eroding and help to keep the rivers flowing. The government agreed to stop the logging.

WHAT YOU CAN DO

● Join a conservation group. Support their work, find out more and even help to protect a rare bird or animal.

● Collect a few acorns and conkers in the autumn. Plant them in your garden, at school or in a patch of wasteland. Take care of them and watch them grow.

● Start a paper recycling or tree planting scheme at school or where you live.

● Encourage your family to buy environment friendly and recycled products.

BOMBO MEETS MOTHER EAGLE

For thousands of years people have told stories about the world around them. These often try to explain something that people do not understand. This tale is told by the Iroquois people of America's Eastern forests.

Bombo was a great hunter. He lived deep in the forests of Pennsylvania and caught more deer than any hunter his people had ever known. Every morning he set out with his special green bow and his long, sharp arrows. Every lunchtime he returned with a deer slung over his shoulder.

Bombo had magic power. All he had to do was call to the deer and they would come and graze near his home. But he was not satisfied. He wanted more.

One day he decided to test his power. He called to the eagles, "Hey, Eagles, I have fresh meat here for you. Come and take it to your eeries." Golden eagles swooped down from all directions. There were males, females, even some young ones who had only just learned to fly. But as they reached the feast, Bombo shot them one by one and stole their feathers.

The next day, Bombo called the eagles again. Eighteen female birds glided majestically down to find food for their chicks. He aimed his arrow and was just about to shoot when a voice behind him said, "Stop!" Bombo swung round in surprise. Standing before him was his best friend, Lilo.

"This is very dangerous, Bombo," he warned. "You must stop immediately. The animals are upset and angry. It is wrong to shoot the eagles and take their feathers."

"Nonsense," replied Bombo. "I'm not doing any harm. Look at my beautiful feather collection. I can make some amazing arrows now."

"You're wrong," said Lilo. "I'm your friend and I don't want to see you hurt, but if you don't stop, the animals will teach you a lesson."

But Bombo ignored his friend and walked off, shaking his head.

The next day Bombo called the eagles for the third time. To his surprise, nothing happened. The forest remained silent and still. As Bombo strained his ears for some sound from the eagles, he thought that he could hear a faint humming. Suddenly, a gigantic dark shape loomed out of the sky towards him. It was the Mother of all Eagles — and she was very, very angry. Bombo had never been so terrified in his life. He took one look at her and ran off as fast as he could. He spotted a hollow log and quickly wriggled inside, but Mother Eagle was just behind him. She grabbed him with her huge claws and swept him up into the air with two angry beats of her powerful wings.

They flew up and up until the forest looked like a green carpet below them. Bombo's heart was beating faster and faster. He felt dizzy. The forest seemed to turn from green to blue. Mother Eagle swooped up and down and around in circles until Bombo thought he would die. As they soared up again, he thought he glimpsed the edge of the forest way below. He panicked. Were they about to leave his home altogether?

All of a sudden, they were heading straight for a huge tree. Just as Bombo was sure they were going to crash, Mother Eagle swooped down into her eerie, dropped him into her nest with her chicks and flew off.

Bombo was terrified. However would he get home now? Suddenly he had an idea. In his pocket he had some dried meat and leather thongs. He offered the meat to the eaglets, who gobbled it up greedily, then he tied their beaks with the thongs.

When Mother Eagle came back with food for her chicks and saw what Bombo had done, she was furious.

"This is wrong, Bombo. Untie them this minute," she cried.

"No," replied Bombo. "I won't untie them until you promise to let me go."

For two days Mother Eagle tried to unpick the tight leather thongs with her sharp beak, but to no avail. Meanwhile, her chicks grew thinner and thinner. They were soon so weak that they could hardly stand up. Mother Eagle flew off around the forest with a grave look on her face.

Finally, she returned to the nest. "I'll make a pact with you, Bombo," she said. "If you promise never to kill another eagle without permission from the Spirit World and if you untie my chicks this minute, you may go back to your home safely."

"I promise," he replied, untying the thongs so that the hungry chicks could eat at last. As Mother Eagle fed her family, Bombo saw them grow big and strong right before his eyes. Suddenly, before he could even blink, he found himself back, safe and sound, in his own home.

From that day on, whenever Bombo caught a deer he called the eagles and invited them to come and share the meal in safety. He never killed another eagle and the only feathers he collected were the ones the eagles left for him. From then on, all the hunters in the forest followed Bombo's example. The eagles and the forest people understood one another at last.

TRUE OR FALSE?

Which of these facts are true and which ones are false? If you have read this book carefully, you will know the answers.

1. Most woodlands are in the top half of the world.

2. Beavers warn their family of trouble by thumping their feet and slapping their tails.

3. Stoats have a white coat in summer and a brown one in winter.

4. Nuthatches stand upside down on tree trunks to catch insects.

5. A woodpecker has such a long tongue that it has to keep it curled up inside its head.

6. Waxwings have bright red feathers to attract a mate.

7. If a wolf is attacked, its tail can drop off to allow it to escape.

8. Indian women saved their forest by hugging the trees.

9. Rabbits have special skin flaps so that they can fly through the forest.

10. Maori people used pine trees to make their war canoes.

GLOSSARY

Acid rain is rain polluted by chemicals released from industrial waste, car exhausts and burning fuel. It can poison trees and plants and erode the face of buildings.

Altitude is the measurement of height above sea level.

Arid land is parched soil with sparse vegetation. Little rain falls on this type of land and it is prone to desertification.

An **avalanche** is caused when heavy snow slips down a mountainside. It can damage property and injure people and animals.

Bay is a part of an ocean or other large body of water that forms a curve in the shoreline. It is bordered on the coastline by headlands or capes.

Block mountains are formed when a block of rock is forced up a crack, or fault, in the Earth's crust. It often has a flat surface on top, similar to a plain, called a plateau.

Bushmen are people who live in desert lands such as in Africa or Australia. They drink little, as they obtain enough moisture from eating underground roots and desert melons.

Camouflage hides animals against their surroundings to protect them from predators, and can help them capture prey.

Carnivores are animals that eat other animals. Herbivores only eat plants. Omnivores eat both meat and plants.

Coniferous trees produce cones, and are evergreen. They are found mainly in the northern hemisphere.

Conservation is the protection and preservation of wildlife and the environment in which it lives.

A **continent** is a large piece of land, or mainland. It is larger than a normal island and is usually divided into several countries (except for the continent of Australia). Two or more continents may be joined together by a narrow neck of land.

A **coral reef** is a colourful ridge formation, usually underwater. It is made up of the hard outer casing produced by a colony of millions of tiny animals known as polyps.

The **core** is the centre of the Earth. It is thought to be solid and is likely to be made of iron and nickel.

Courtship display is when a bird, animal or insect performs specially or changes colour to attract a mate.

The **crust** is the Earth's thin surface layer. Mountains are built in the crust.

A **current** or stream is the movement of a body of water in a particular direction. Ocean currents may be strong and extend over great distances.

Deciduous trees lose all of their leaves before a cold or dry season. They cannot live in very cold climates, unlike coniferous trees. They are known as deciduous or broadleaved trees.

Deforestation is the destruction of large areas of woodland to make room for building, mining or farming.

A **desert** is a place with little vegetation where less than 10 inches (25 centimetres) of rain falls each year.

Desertification is the process by which dry areas of land on the edge of deserts suffer from drought and also become desert. If regular rainfall returns to the area, the new region of desert could recover.

Domesticated animals are those which have been bred by humans over many generations to be tame and, in some cases, to provide products such as meat, milk, leather and wool.

A **drought** is a period when little or no rain falls. Crops do not grow, water is scarce, and animals and humans find it hard to survive.

An **echo** is the repetition of a noise caused by the bouncing back of sound waves from a solid object. Marine mammals such as dolphins use echoes to locate food and to avoid obstacles.

An **ecosystem** is a community of plants and animals and their environment.

The **environment** is the set of conditions in the area where an animal lives. The animal's survival depends on how well it can respond to these conditions.

Ephemerals are tiny plants that survive as seeds in dry conditions such as deserts. During a period of heavy rain they burst into flower.

The **Equator** is the imaginary line around the Earth, exactly halfway between the North and South Poles.

Erosion is the wearing away of soil or land by wind or water. Trees help to prevent erosion.

Evaporation is when water turns into tiny droplets of vapour in the air. This process happens each morning to the dew that has fallen during the night in the hot desert.

Evergreen trees replace their leaves throughout the year. This means that they always look green.

Extinction occurs when the last member of an animal or plant species dies out. This may be due to overhunting by humans, a change in habitat, or a failure to compete with a new animal or plant.

Famine is a period when food is scarce and many people and animals starve and die. This often takes place after a drought, when crops have been unable to grow.

Fertile land is land which is good for growing lush and healthy crops.

Fold mountains are formed when rock is crumpled and forced upwards as the edges of some of the Earth's plates meet and grind together.

A **gulf** is a part of a sea or ocean that loops into the neighbouring coastline. It has a narrower mouth than a bay.

A **habitat** is the natural environment of a plant or animal.

Hibernate is what some animals do in cold weather to survive. They fatten themselves during the warmer months, then sleep all through the long winter. While hibernating, animals use little energy and many do not need food.

Hunter-gatherers are people who live off the land by harvesting food from the plants and animals that live there. They are skilful in taking only what the land can survive without.

Irrigation is the method by which farmers water land that naturally tends to be dry. Water is often channelled over land through ditches or retained on land with a hard, resistant surface such as low walls.

Land-locked bodies of water are surrounded by land.

Larvae are the young of some insect species before they develop and grow wings.

Latitude is a line drawn from east to west on a map.

The **mantle** is the layer of rock surrounding the Earth's core, lying beneath the crust.

Marine means related to the sea. Marine animals are those that live in the sea.

To **migrate** is to travel long distances every year. Many birds migrate from summer breeding grounds to warmer winter feeding places.

A **mineral** is a chemical compound found in rocks. Some minerals are useful to humans and are mined.

Mixed woodlands are forests with evergreen conifers as well as seasonal deciduous trees.

A **native** is a plant, animal or person whose family originally comes from the area in which it lives.

Nomads are people who travel from one area to another, either to take their herds of animals to fresh grazing or to escape severe weather, such as cold or drought. They feed mainly on products from their herds and live in tents, which can easily be packed up and carried on the next journey.

A **pearl** is a small gem, usually round and white, cream, or bluish-grey. It slowly forms as a protective layer around a grain of sand or other object that irritates the soft flesh inside an oyster's shell.

Pesticides are chemicals used to kill pests that feed on crops. Pesticides may sometimes be dangerous to creatures other than the pests they control.

Plankton is the rich 'soup' in bodies of water made up of many types of microscopic life. A large variety of sea animals feeds on it.

Plates are the huge slabs of rock which make up the Earth's crust.

A **plateau** is the flat area at the top of a block mountain.

The **Poles** are found at the exact north and south ends of the Earth. Day and night each last six months at the Poles.

To **pollute** means to poison air, land or water. Pollution is often caused by the waste from human industrial activity.

A **pollutant** is a dirty and poisonous product such as car fumes that damages the environment.

Predators are animals that hunt and kill other creatures.

Rainforests are thick, evergreen forests with high levels of rainfall. Temperate rainforests are warm and moist with most rainfall in winter. Tropical rainforests are hot and wet with heavy rainfall all year round.

Rain shadow is the area on a mountainside facing away from the sea. It receives little rain. Most of the rain falls over the seaward side of the mountain.

Reproduction is when adult creatures produce new, young individuals for the continuation of their species.

Resources are the natural materials taken from their environment and used by people, for example, wood.

Rodents are small mammals, such as squirrels and beavers, with strong front teeth which they use for gnawing hard objects.

Scrubland is territory where vegetation grows low and stunted.

Snowline is the level on the side of a mountain above which no plant life can grow. Snow often covers the mountain above this level all the year round.

Species is a group of animals or plants that share the same characteristics and can breed with one another.

Taproots are long, thin roots that push their way through the layers of stone beneath the sand. They help some desert trees find moisture during long periods of drought.

Territory is the area where an animal lives and breeds.

Tides are the regular rise and fall of the sea, caused by the pull of the Moon and the Sun.

Topsoil is the uppermost and richest layer of earth where most plants grow. Desert topsoil has dried out and blown away due to lack of rain.

Toxic means poisonous and harmful to life.

Treeline is the level on a mountainside above which the climate is too cold and windy for trees to grow.

A **trench** is a deep furrow. The Mariana Trench near Guam is the deepest known place in any ocean.

Tropic of Cancer and **Tropic of Capricorn** are imaginary lines at about 23°27"north and south of the Equator. Most deserts are found along these two lines.

Tubers are short, thick parts of underground stems of certain plants. They are covered in small bumps.

Volcanoes are openings in the Earth's crust from which hot, molten rock and gas may leak and cover the surrounding land.

Wildwoods are ancient woodlands in their natural state, inhabited by their original species.

Woodlands are areas of land in temperate countries, where many trees grow close together.

INDEX

NOTES

NOTES

NOTES